To Mummi

Lots of lov

from

Diane xxx

OTHER HELEN EXLEY GIFTBOOKS:
Thanks Dad!
Thank you to a real friend
To a very special Mother
To a lovely Mother

Printed simultaneously in 2007 by Helen Exley Giftbooks in Great Britain
and Helen Exley Giftbooks LLC in the USA.

12  11  10  9  8  7

Illustrations © Emma Davis 2007
Pam Brown © Helen Exley 2007
Copyright © Helen Exley 2007

Printed in China

ISBN-13: 978-1-905130-71-9

Pictures by Emma Davis, from the Soul Happiness collection
Words by Pam Brown
Edited by Helen Exley

Helen Exley Giftbooks, 16 Chalk Hill, Watford, Herts WD19 4BG, UK.
**www.helenexleygiftbooks.com**

# Thank you Mum
# For everything

BY PAM BROWN
PICTURES BY EMMA DAVIS

A HELEN EXLEY GIFTBOOK

# HOME

You have made a home for us
in the midst of the world's tumult
– a place of certainty,
a place of welcome.

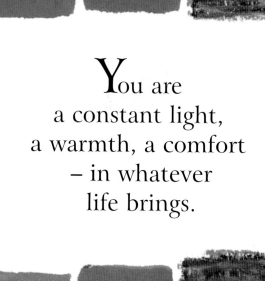

You are
a constant light,
a warmth, a comfort
– in whatever
life brings.

You are always there,
my Pole Star –
however distant, however
hidden by dark clouds.
Unwavering in kindness and concern –
certainty in an uncertain world.

# CHILDHOOD

*You created the scent*
*of childhood*
*– hot strawberry jam,*
*new bread, soap, geraniums,*
*clean sheets, lavender, toffee.*
*Thank you Mum.*

# MAGIC!

You have taken most ordinary things
and made of them astonishments.
Thank you for the magic of childhood.

SENSIBLE MOTHERS
LET THEIR
CHILDREN SLEEP.
MOTHERS LIKE YOU
TAKE THEM
OUT OF BED
TO SEE A SHOWER
OF FALLING STARS.

For all the laughter,
all the hugs
all the lovely, crazy things
we did together.
For all the kisses that took away
the aches and pains.
For all the small treats,
all the homely pattern of my days.
For all the happiness you gave.
Thank you, Mum.

*Thank you*
*for those happy,*
*happy days*
*– and for all*
*that I am,*
*and hope for.*

# FOR MY LIFE

Thank you for giving me life
– for the chance to watch great waves
breaking along the shore,
to hear the shout of birdsong
in the dawn, to hold my hands
beneath running water,
to smell grass after rain,
to taste fresh bread.
For the gifts of friendship, laughter
and creativity.

# Feeling
# Wanted

Thank you
for making me feel
wanted, precious,
irreplaceable.

Thank you
for fitting your life to ours.
Thank you for
making us feel that
nothing that you have achieved
is worth more than our love.

THANK YOU
FOR YOUR WILD
DELIGHT
WHEN I SUCCEED.

Thanks for getting into my head
that I am absolutely unique,
that there has never,
since the world began,
been a person just like me.

# Care

For your care when I was small.
For your gentleness when I was sick.
For your patience and forgiveness
when I behaved so badly.
For your sittings-up until
my key was in the door.
For your strength and your
encouragement when I was in distress.
For your faith in me.
Your love for me.

# SO CONFIDENT
# IN ME

You seem always, so sure,
so confident that I will come through.
But I know how often
you have lain awake,
living through everything I suffer.
"Thank you" is so inadequate.
But it is all I can find to say.
And that I love you.

Thank you for understanding
when I came across something
I simply couldn't do,
however hard I tried.

Understand algebra, hold a tune,
conquer my fear of heights.
Don't worry, you said.
Enjoy the things you can do.

# STRENGTH AND
# YOUR COURAGE

Somehow mothers find strength
and wisdom they never knew
they possessed.
Somehow they become, quietly
and unobtrusively, the keystones
of our lives.
This is to thank them all – and you –
for that courage, patience,
kindness, understanding.

# Trust

Thank you for telling me
what I already knew in my heart,
but calmly, clearly, positively.
So that I could take it from there.

# FOR YOUR

Everyone needs a mother
to cheer when things go right.
It's good to have the applause
of friends, family and colleagues –
but one looks above
their heads, to make sure your
mother is clapping!

# APPLAUSE

# ANYTHING

Thank you for being ready
to lend anything, give anything
that will help us through.
Thank you for always being
ready to help.

Thank you for all the sewing-up
of rips and hanging hems,
the polishing of scuffs,
the sponging out of stains.
Thank you for all the liniment,
the sticking plasters, the linctus.
The cuddles. The kisses.
The holding of hands in thunderstorms.

# SACRIFICE

Thank you for the sleepless nights,
the anxious days
and the financial nightmares
that were part and parcel
of my childhood.
But about which I knew nothing –
I only knew the happiness of your love
and the certainty of your care.

Enduring my

crazes!

Thank you for enduring my vivariums.
Ants and worms and wood lice.
And their frequent escapings.

Thank you for showing
such an intelligent interest in my frogs,
my bead collection, my grazes,
my loose tooth
and my playing of the recorder.

# A LIFETIME OF

# LITTLE THINGS

The meals. Hundreds of them.
Thousands of them.
An Everest of crockery and glass.
The laundry basket that filled
as it was emptied – like a fairy tale.

...all the little things,
the ordinary things I took
for granted; trivial when seen
day by day, but mounting up
to mind-boggling statistics over
those years of childhood.

# For forgiving me

Frazzled nerves,
sleepless nights, spoiled dinners,
plans destroyed, worn carpets.
Green hair, black fingernails.
All the disappointments
and disasters, large and small,
I've scattered in my wake.
Thank you for forgiving me.

When I was small
my little bony hands were
anchored in yours
whenever danger threatened –
wherever there was something
grand to see – whenever
we were scampering toward
a new adventure.
Now they meet as hands of
companions and friends.
But holding a lifetime of loving
in their touch.

We have loved
each other
since the beginning
– love each other still.
And forever.

# You were there

– close by when I was very small
and still within reach,
however far time and circumstance
have divided us.
I have only to reach for you
– and you are there.

Thank you for the laughter,
the cuddles.
The chases. The fun.
Thank you for so much happiness.
So much tenderness.
So much love.

*The*

*laughter*

# With you

It's strange.
Mothers chat and laugh
with you on the telephone
– but if you tell them
something is most terribly wrong,
suddenly they are there
with you in the room.

There may be a hundred miles
between you,
but their arms are round
your shoulders.
And what seemed shapeless
and overwhelming is
– something you can deal with.

# TRANSFORMED
# BY LOVE

Little children do not classify
their mothers as people.
They are another species.
It takes us a life-time to discover
our mothers were simply human beings,
transformed by love.
And knowing this
we are, at last, able to say thank you.

# Love lies

Thank you for never letting me know
my cuddle blanket had been
through the wash.
That Teddy was not the dearly-loved
bear left on a train.

That the skylark did not sing
just for me.
That you had cried in secret
over the broken bowl...
Lies perhaps – but golden lies –
that lasted just long enough
to let me grow and be happy.

# Holding

Your hugs healed bruises, scuffs
and scratches,
drove away misery,
restored hope,
crowned victories,
comforted a broken heart.

m e

And even now,
I feel your arms around me still,
steadying me
and giving me comfort.

# Bedtime

"See, no dragons
underneath the bed.
Sleep now." you said.
"Safe and sound till morning –
I'm never far away."
And so I drifted into sleep,
wrapped in your love.

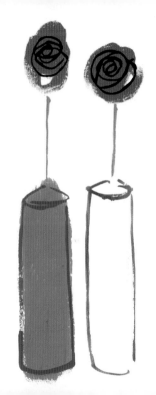

# Anchor

You are the very roots
of my existence.
Life may buffet me
– but I will not fall.
You anchor me. You steady me.
You give me the strength
to endure.

# THROUGH
# THE LOW TIMES

Thank you for putting up
with temper, defiance, laziness.
Noise and untidiness.
Stupidity and showings-off.
All the battery of awfulness a child
employs to see how far it is
allowed to go.
You stood your ground.
You went on loving me.

*Don't think
I don't know how hard
it has been for you
sometimes.
It makes my
gratitude the deeper.*

# you

You made hard times
seem good times.

# Your love

Mothers endure every illness,
every grief, every anxiety suffered
by their children
– often powerless to help.
Only able to wait, to love.
Thank you – for that love
is what I hold on to.

# LESSONS IN LOVE

Even now, I can still feel my hand
safe in your hand,
the softness of your cheek,
the hug that headed off sorrow,
the kiss that healed all pain.
Held in memory so vivid that they
have never faded.
You taught me how to love. Thank you.

You held me close.
You set me on my feet
and steadied me, encouraged me,
guided me,
until the day you gently
let go my hands
and let me walk alone.

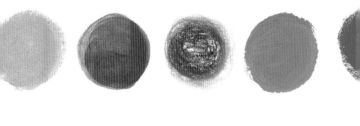

# Memories

Thank you for the golden days.

Thank you
for a thousand
good memories
on which
I've built my life.

# MY STRENGTH

You are my strength,
my treasure
 and my friend –
the rock that has endured
 through all
  the shifting years.
My dear, my dearest mother.
Thank you.

*If you love this book...*

...look out for other Helen Exley Giftbooks. There are over 300 thoughtful gift ideas listed on our website. There is something for mothers, daughters and other members of the family, and for friends. Here are just some of our other 'Mother' gifts:

The Love Between Mothers and Sons
The Love Between Mothers and Daughters
Words of love about Mothers
Go Girl!
Women's Quotations

*And a few of our other top books...*

Taking Time to Just Be
To a very special Husband
The Great Gift of Love
A Woman's Work is Never Done
Happy day!
Sorry
To a very special Grandma

Visit Helen Exley's website to see the full list of titles:
**www.helenexleygiftbooks.com**

# What is a Helen Exley Giftbook?

*Helen Exley Giftbooks* cover the most powerful range of all human relationships: love between couples, the bonds within families and between friends.

No expense is spared in making sure that each book is as thoughtful and meaningful a gift as it is possible to create: good to give, good to receive.

You have the result in your hands. If you have loved it – please tell others! There is no power on earth like the word-of-mouth recommendation of friends.

**Helen Exley Giftbooks**
16 Chalk Hill, Watford, WD19 4BG, UK,
www.helenexleygiftbooks.com